Frederick Douglass

Leader Against Slavery

Patricia and Fredrick McKissack

Illustrated by Ned O.

❖ *Great African Americans Series* ❖

ENSLOW PUBLISHERS, INC.

Bloy St. & Ramsey Ave. P.O. Box 38
Box 777 Aldershot
Hillside, N.J. 07205 Hants GU12 6BP
U.S.A. U.K.

To Blake

Library of Congress Cataloging-in-Publication Data

McKissack, Pat, 1944–
    Frederick Douglass: leader against slavery/Patricia and
Fredrick McKissack; illustrated by Ned O.
        p. cm. — (Great African Americans series)
    Includes index.
    Summary: Simple text and illustrations describe the life and
accomplishments of this famous abolitionist.
    ISBN 0-89490-306-3
    1. Douglass, Frederick, 1817?–1895—Juvenile literature.
2. Abolitionists—United States—Biography—Juvenile literature.
3. Afro-Americans—Biography—Juvenile literature. 4. Slavery—
United States—Anti-slavery movements—Juvenile literature.
[1. Douglass, Frederick, 1817?–1895. 2. Abolitionists. 3. Afro-
Americans—Biography.] I. McKissack, Fredrick. II. Ostendorf,
Edward, ill. III. Title. IV. Series: McKissack, Pat, 1944– Great
African Americans series.
E449.D75M378 1991
973.8'092—dc20
[B]   91-3084
                               CIP
                               AC

Printed in the United States of America

10 9 8 7 6 5 4 3 2 1

Photo Credits: Library of Congress, pp. 18, 20, 24, 26, 27, 28; Missouri Histori-
cal Society, pp. 7, 23; Moorland-Spingarn Research Center, Howard University,
pp. 4, 14, 16.

Illustration Credits: Ned O., pp. 6, 8, 9, 10, 12, 17, 27.
Cover Illustration: Ned O.

Contents

Frederick Douglass
Born: February 14, 1817(?), Tuckahoe, Maryland.
Died: February 20, 1895, Washington, D.C.

1

Alone!

Harriet Bailey was a **slave**.* All of her
children were slaves too. On (or near)
Valentine's Day in about 1817, Harriet
gave birth to a son. She named him
Frederick Augustus Washington Bailey.

When the baby was only one week old,
Harriet was ordered back to work. But
Frederick wasn't left alone. He was sent

---

* Words in **bold type** are explained in *Words to Know* on page 30.

to live with his Grandmama Betsey and Grandpa Isaac.

Little Fred didn't see his mother very much. She worked far away. Fred was happy until he was about eight years old.

At that time Grandmama Betsey took him to the main **plantation**, in Tuckahoe, Maryland. She had been told to leave him there. Why, Why? he cried.

The boy didn't understand slavery. Slaves had to do what their **masters** said.

The cook took care of all the children at the main plantation. She was a slave too. Still, she beat Fred when he cried.

One day the cook was going to beat Fred. But Harriet came in. "Never hit my child again," the angry mother said. The cook ran away.

As if they were animals, people were sold in public places to be slaves. The person who offered the most money bought the slave. Men, women, and children were sold this way for almost 250 years in the United States.

Harriet hugged her son. She fed him. She sang to him. Then it was time for her to go. Harriet had to do what her master said.

Fred never saw his mother again. Harriet died soon after that visit.

Fred was alone!

2

Never!

Fred lived at the main plantation for a year. The cook beat him almost every day.

Then Fred was sent to be a **houseboy** for Sophia and Hugh Auld.

Sophia Auld was a kind woman. She taught her son and Fred how to read and write.

Then one day Fred read for Mr. Auld. Mr. Auld was very, very angry. "Never teach a slave to read," said Mr. Auld. "He won't want to stay a slave."

Mrs. Auld stopped teaching Fred how to read. But Fred didn't stop reading.

When Fred was sixteen, he was sent back to the main plantation in Tuckahoe. Thomas Auld was his master.

Fred wouldn't act like a slave. So Auld sent him to a **slave-breaker**. He was made to work from morning until night. All he had to do was act like a slave. But Fred

said "Never!" He stayed with the slave-breaker for almost a year.

One day Fred fought back. He stopped the slave-breaker from beating him. Auld and the slave-breaker had tried to make Fred a willing slave. Now they knew it would never work.

Thomas Auld sent Frederick back to Hugh and Sophia. By that time, Fred knew that he was going to run away.

Frederick helped build and fix ships. Many of his friends were free. Frederick knew he would live as a free man one day.

3

Run!

It was 1838. Frederick was eighteen years old and very good-looking.

He met Anna, a free black woman who lived in Baltimore, Maryland. He loved Anna and wanted to marry her. But Frederick wouldn't ask—not until he was free, too.

Freedom was always on his mind. He wanted to run! Run! Run! His friends said wait. He needed a plan.

After many months of planning,

Frederick was ready to run. At last the day came. Dressed as a free sailor, he rode the train to Delaware. Blacks who were not slaves had to carry **free papers** all the time. Frederick's free papers belonged to a friend. If anyone checked, he was in trouble. But no one checked closely.

From Delaware, Frederick took a boat to Philadelphia. Run, Fred, run!

Anna and Fred were married in New York. Their children were Rosetta, Lewis Henry, Frederick, Jr., Charles, and Annie. Annie died when she was very young.

From Philadelphia, he went to New York. Run, Fred, run!

On September 4, 1838, Frederick was in a **free state**. He changed his name to Frederick Augustus Douglass.

Right away, he sent for Anna. They were married in New York. Soon, the happy couple moved to New Bedford,

Runaway slaves could be forced to go back to their masters. Douglass changed his name so slave catchers would have a hard time finding him.

Massachusetts. Frederick got a job working on ships.

It didn't take long for Fred to join the **abolitionists**. These were people who wanted to end slavery.

Frederick spoke out against slavery all over the North. He even wrote his own life story.

Then he had to run again. **Slave hunters** would be coming to take him back to his master. Run! Run!

Fred said good-bye to his wife and children. Then he hurried off to England.

Two years later, on December 5, 1846, Frederick was truly freed. Friends had bought his freedom. He came back to the United States in 1847 with his own free papers. He never had to run again.

Douglass believed the only way slavery would end was through war. Some abolitionists agreed with him. Some did not.

4

Freedom!

Frederick Douglass was a free man. But what about all those who were still slaves? He believed all people should be free. That would be his life's work.

The Douglasses moved to Rochester, New York. There, Frederick opened the *North Star*, a weekly newspaper. The North Star was the light in the sky that **runaways** followed to freedom.

Abraham Lincoln was elected **President** of the United States in

November 1860. South Carolina said it was no longer a part of the United States in December 1860. Other states in the South followed. The **Civil War** began in April 1861. In 1863 Lincoln freed the slaves.

Douglass wept when he heard the news. "What (Lincoln) has done is to (get rid of) a terrible evil that has (had hold of) this country. . . ."

Douglass met with President Lincoln in the **White House**. Douglass asked that black men be allowed to join the North's army. They had the right to fight for freedom.

Douglass's two sons were among the first black men to join the **Union Army.** Other black men followed. The African-American soldiers won many medals for **bravery** during the war.

Later Douglass pushed for equal pay. "Black and white soldiers die the same," he said. They should be paid the same. At last, both black and white soldiers were paid the same.

The war ended in 1865. President Lincoln was killed soon afterwards. Douglass was very sad. He said, "It is a dark time for us all."

Above, black soldiers fight and die at Fort Wagner. Douglass pushed for black soldiers to get the same pay as white soldiers. He also pushed for better medical treatment.

After the Civil War, Douglass closed the *North Star*. But his work was not over.

5

Hero!

When the Civil War ended, Frederick Douglass was called a hero. He had not been a soldier. But he had been fighting to end slavery for so long.

Some people thought Douglass' work was over. Instead, he tried new things. For a while he was president of a bank. And he also worked for women's rights.

Finally, the Douglasses closed the *North Star* and moved to **Washington, D.C.** President Rutherford B. Hayes had asked Douglass to be the **marshal of the District of Columbia**. He was chosen by other presidents to serve the **government** too.

The Douglass home was called Cedar Hill. It was a happy place. People came to visit all the time. Anna always made their house a fun place. Their children were

Douglass's sons Lewis Henry (left), Frederick Jr.(right), and Charles fought in the Civil War. His grandson, Joseph Douglass (center), became the first African-American violinist to make concert tours.

grown up. They had children of their own. It was full of happy sounds and good smells. Douglass was never too busy to hug a grandchild. Family was always very important to him.

Anna died after being ill. Once more Frederick was alone. He had never liked being alone. Soon he married a second time. Many people felt he should not have married again. But he was happy.

Frederick Douglass often took part in programs honoring
Civil War soldiers and sailors.

But Frederick was not happy about the way things were changing. By the 1890s, unfair laws were being passed. Black people were losing their rights. Frederick Douglass was old and tired. But he still spoke up for freedom and justice. He always would.

He spoke to a large group in Washington, D.C. on February 20, 1895. Later that evening, Frederick Douglass died. A great American hero was gone.

Douglass will always be remembered as an abolitionist. He had been a slave. But he could never understand how one person could own another.

In a speech he gave one Fourth of July, he said, "There is no way a nation can call itself free and accept slavery." We know now that his words are true.

Words to Know

abolitionist (ab-uh-LISH-uh-nist)—A person who was against slavery and wanted to end it in the United States.

bravery—An act that shows courage. Standing up to fear.

Civil War—A war fought within one country. In the United States, the Civil War was fought between states in the North and South.

freedom—The power to make choices and decisions with responsibility.

free papers—Papers showing that a person was not owned.

free state—A state that did not allow slavery.

government—A group that runs a country.

houseboy—A young servant who does chores around the house for his master.

marshal of the District of Columbia—A law officer of the capital of the United States of America.

master—A ruler or a person who controls another. Someone who owns slaves is called a master.

plantation (plan-TAY-shun)—A very large farm.

president (PREZ-i-dent)—The leader of a country or group.

runaway—A slave who ran away to the North where he or she could live in freedom.

slave—A person who is owned by another. That person can be bought or sold.

slave-breaker—Someone hired to work and beat a slave so he or she would obey or fear a master.

slave hunter—Someone who, for money, looked for runaway slaves and took them back to their masters.

Union Army—The army that fought for the North in the Civil War.

Washington, D.C.—The place where the United States capital is located. D.C. stands for District of Columbia.

White House—The house where the President of the United States lives.

Index

DI